CREATIVE ANSWERS TO MISBEHAVIOR

Getting Out Of The
Ignore-Nag-Yell-Punish Cycle

A Family Power Booklet
by
John F. Taylor, Ph.D.

Illustrated by Gregory Griffith

ABOUT THE AUTHOR

John F. Taylor, Ph.D. is a family psychologist in private practice in Salem, Oregon. Married and the father of eight children, this outstanding psychologist and author is nationally known for his seminars on the subject of hyperactivity. For many years he wrote an award-winning column on family relationships and mental health for *The Oregon Statesman*. He writes the "Sharpening Your Counseling Skills" column for the journal *Practical Ideas for Counselors* and has published numerous articles in other professional journals.

Family Power Series Books:

Correcting Without Criticizing
Creative Answers to Misbehavior
Encouraging the Discouraged Child
Helping Hands and Smiling Faces
Listening for Feelings
No More Sibling Rivalry

FAMILY POWER

Reprinted 2003

Table of Contents

Introduction

What can a parent or supervising adult do other than ignore, give a time-out to, lecture, or punish the misbehaving child? Unfortunately these four tools are all that are in many parents' tool boxes for dealing with misbehavior in their children. In this book are some humane and effective alternatives that strengthen the bonds of mutual respect between the child and the supervising adult. The approaches given here are tools, not weapons. Their purpose is to provide something other than the "I'll-get-you" style of child discipline. To make these methods handy and usable, each principle is illustrated by specific word-for-word examples. These principles apply regardless of the age of the child, the presence or absence of psychiatric difficulties, and the nature and severity of misbehavior.

Creative Ways to Confront
the Child About Misbehavior

Once misbehavior occurs, the first step is to break up the scene and confront the child. Unfortunately many parents, teachers, and child care supervisors use poor methods of confrontation that do more harm than good and propel the child into further misbehavior. Confrontation does not need to be harsh, critical, or angry. In fact it ideally should be none of those; instead, it should be supportive and instructive for the child. There seldom should be a need to proceed further than verbal confrontation in order to get a child to stop misbehaving and substitute better behavior in the future.

Of course you will be frustrated, dismayed, confused, disappointed or angry when the child misbehaves. If your composure falls below a certain level, however, you should delay your response until you can calm down somewhat. When you are too angry, your discipline attempt will backfire on you. The ultimate purpose of discipline is instruction in proper behavior, not parent's revenge on the child. Instruction, however, is not what happens when you are too enraged. Instead, you will succeed in little more than getting temporary revenge on the child and setting into motion a chain of events with unfortunate consequences for you and the child. Wise and effective confronting of a misbehaving child requires a certain level of self-control by the adult. It is crucial to avoid a "parent tantrum":

"I'm too angry with you right now."

"We'll talk about this later, after I've had a chance to calm down."

"I'm taking a brisk walk before I talk with you about what you did. Right now I'm too angry."

An important element to setting the stage for more effective confronting of the child about misbehavior involves smoothing the process of communication. It ensures that both of you are sufficiently calm, flexible, and attentive so that your confrontation has the best chance of being helpful to the child. In an auto race the drivers pull into the pit to renew the car and assess how it is doing. In a similar fashion, be willing to interrupt whatever you are doing and have a psychological pit stop in the "race" of dealing with the child. The purpose is to confront about negative processes that are occurring:

> *"Stop for a moment, please. Do you realize what we're saying to each other here? Let's both calm down for a few moments before we continue this conversation."*

 or

> *"Wait a minute! Let's both agree right now to stop this tone of voice we're both using and speak more calmly and courteously to each other."*

USE A SPECIAL SETTING

One way to make confrontation go better is to increase its importance by arranging a special setting. It is often helpful to choose a neutral territory such as a restaurant. This type of arrangement sends a message of urgency and importance that magnifies the impact of your confrontation. Arrange to step aside from distractions when confronting the child about misbehavior:

> *"I have some things to talk about with you. We haven't had our special time this week yet. Let's go to the pizza restaurant where we can have a fun lunch at the same time."*

❖ or ❖

> *"We need to talk, and we need a place where the phone won't keep interrupting us. Come out to the back yard with me and sit for a while on the swing."*

Setting the stage for confrontation involves filling up the child's love "gas tank." To the extent that the child is reminded of the adult's love, the child will be open to confrontation. Put your arm around the child, hold the child in your lap, gently rock the child, and in any other reasonable way use as much affectionate contact and gentle movement as possible:

> *"I'm in the rocking chair. Come sit on my lap, honey. I know this is a hard time for you."*

> *"I know this is a hard time for you; sit next to me so I can rub your back."*

USE A CONCERNS NOTEBOOK

A very effective and powerful tool for preventing misbehavior stemming from the child's built-up anger and frustration is a Concerns Notebook. The child has a special notebook
or journal for troublesome issues, problems, and frustrations.
If the child is too young to write personal entries, the adult or
an older child can write in the Concerns Notebook for the
child. All items are routinely discussed in a special problem-
solving meeting with the adult. In this way, frustrations are
dealt with in their early stages, before they develop into major
problems, anger explosions, or misbehavior by the child:

> *"If you don't like how I handled this situation*
> *between you and Andrew, write it down in your*
> *Concerns Notebook and we'll discuss it later."*

❖ *or* ❖

> *"Tara's problems with your noise should be*
> *discussed between you and me. Can you please*
> *write that down in your Concerns Notebook so*
> *we won't forget?"*

7

To make the Concerns Notebook method even more powerful, guarantee the child a regular "day in court" about the concerns written in it. During these meetings, called Personal Private Interviews (PPI's), make it safe for the child to express all concerns or frustrations. Avoid criticizing the child and have these PPI meetings often enough so you can closely track the child's frustrations; once a week is suitable in most families. Of course you won't be able to "solve" everything the child brings up in exactly the way the child wishes, and some issues will simply require the child to make self-changes for the better. But focus on understanding the child's feelings and on making positive changes to improve some of the situations:

> *"Now that we're alone in our own PPI, tell me exactly what bothers you about what happened last night between you and Jeremy. I'll listen, and after I'm sure I understand, we might be able to think of some ways to improve that situation."*

> *"Thank you for writing that down in your Concerns Notebook, because I had forgotten about it. I'll change the alarm setting so you don't have that problem any more in the morning."*

The child will also respond better to confrontation after you listen quietly to the child's explanation of the events involved. Giving the child an opportunity to explain sends a message of acceptance and interest that paves the way for better communication with you. Listen attentively and respectfully to the child's description of the incident:

> *"I can see how mad you are at Sherri. Please tell me exactly what she did so I can understand."*

> *"I can help both of you better if I know exactly what happened. Please tell me what you did and what he did."*

ACKNOWLEDGE THE CHILD'S NEEDS

The child will respond better if you start by acknowledging the child's needfulness behind the misbehavior. Probe to clarify what needs the child was attempting to meet by misbehaving. Then show empathy for the child's plight of being needful in those ways:

> *"Could it be that one reason for these antics in front of us is that you feel overlooked and not paid attention to?"*

> *"When most children act like this, they feel bullied and violated by the other child. Could that be one of your feelings this evening?"*

Children are almost always angry when they misbehave. It is very helpful to acknowledge the child's desperation, frustration, or anger that might be accompanying the misbehavior. The child will accept your confrontation better after this show of empathy for the child's dilemma and desperateness: [1]

> *"I understand how hurt you must feel right now, and how angry you are at Thomas."*

❖ or ❖

> *"The way you hit Joel shows that you're very, very bothered by him now. This is a really hard time for you, isn't it, April!"*

---

[1] For a more detailed discussion of the process of empathy, see another *Family Power Booklet*, *Correcting Without Criticizing*, available from mar*co products, inc.

AFFIRM THE CHILD'S LOVABILITY

It is easy for any child to get "Mom doesn't like what I did" confused with "Mom doesn't love me" and with "I'm not lovable." The last two messages are devastating to the child, and it is important to make sure the child hasn't become confused by these three similar messages. You may want to use a pet as an analogy. Even though the pet may do an occasional irritating thing (a cat that scratches at furniture, or a dog that barks at the wrong time, for example), the child still loves the pet. In the same way, parents still love the child, though the misbehavior must stop. During the confrontation, affirm the child's lovability and your desire to still feel and show love for the child:

> *"We want you to be happy and to enjoy being with your sister during evenings like this one. When you misbehave like this, you can't possibly be happy."*

❖ *or* ❖

> *"You're our special little guy, and we don't want to see you be so upset when things don't go exactly the way you thought they would."*

11

TEACH HOW MISBEHAVIOR HARMS THE CHILD OR OTHERS

The goal of confrontation is to help the child learn how and why to improve behavior. Telling a child to change behavior "because I said so" teaches nothing useful. Misbehavior is not wrong because the child will be penalized, lose points, lose an allowance, be denied privileges, or got caught. It is also not wrong because the adult said so. It is wrong because if it continues it will bring harm of some sort to the child, to others, to property, or to animals. Help the child learn why the misbehavior was wrong in this basic sense, in terms that the child can understand and that go beyond "because I said so":

> *"The reason why I won't allow you to do that to Jared is that he has a right to his privacy, just as you do to your privacy."*

 or ❖

> *"We need that rule in this family because of the way our cats act when anyone starts doing that to them."*

12

Training the child in decision-making helps bring about future improved behavior. Simply telling the child to stop a misbehavior often falls far short of addressing the underlying needs the misbehavior was intended to meet. It is important to give the child a substitute for the misbehavior—a new and better way of behaving that will meet those same needs. Help the child discover what to do as an alternative to misbehavior in future similar situations, either by asking leading questions or by suggesting the new desired behavior:

> *"The next time Sarah bothers you like this, what would be a better thing to do than hit her?"*

or

> *"From now on when you want to play with Steve's drum, ask to borrow it rather than sneaking into his room and taking it without permission."*

Effective solutions to conflicts almost always involve meeting the needs of all involved. One-sided win-lose solutions, in which someone gives in or compromises too much, seldom work. Developing win-win solutions not only solves conflicts here-and-now but helps teach the child how to build effective solutions in the future:

> *"What do you think would make him more content next time so that he wouldn't do that to you and you wouldn't get so mad at him?"*

❖ *or* ❖

> *"I want to find a solution that will make everybody more calm, so this kind of problem won't happen next time."*

Finding win-win solutions also reduces the child's self-centeredness by forcing the addressing of the other person's needs. Practice of this sort is an important building block for the child's problem solving skills. Help the child understand that the wisest way to get others to do whatever the child wants them to do is to make sure their needs are met:

> *"If you want Walt to play catch with you in the future, be sure to throw the ball more gently, so he can feel successful at catching it. That way both of you will enjoy playing catch more."*

❖ or ❖

> *"The real solution to Tara's obnoxious antics is to make sure she doesn't get so bored. Use the Fun Idea List earlier in the evening. As long as her needs are met, she won't bother you."*

Explain the Merits of the Correct Alternative

It is one thing to tell a child what to do next time. It is another to convince the child of the merits of the proposed improved behavior. The best procedure is to explain the common-sense, automatic ripple or domino effects of the correct behavior. This explanation should be in simple, easy-to-understand terms involving a crystal clear logical sequence. The results of the correct behavior should include a "win-win solution" involving the child and other affected persons. Using clear examples, explain why the desired improvements in the child's behavior for future similar situations are better than the misbehavior the child has shown:

> *"If you use the Fun Idea List rather than bug your brother, you and he will both be happier and calmer, and there won't be as much fighting between the two of you."*

❖ *or* ❖

> *"There will be no reason for him to come into your room as long as you handle these situations in the new way we talked about."*

EMPHASIZE FUTURE IMPROVEMENTS

History lessons ("How many times have I told you...") and criticisms refer to the past and destroy self-esteem. An effective confrontation, on the other hand, always builds for improved behavior in the future. Maintain a future-oriented emphasis, rather than a past-oriented emphasis. Refer to the future and the possibilities of improving behavior:

> *"The reason why you just can't keep doing this is that Sherry won't want to play with you the next time she comes over."*

 or

> *"What can we do differently next week so that we don't go through this same problem about your chores?"*

Effective Disciplinary Responses to Misbehavior

Often simply confronting the child will prevent a repeat of misbehavior. When a stronger consequence seems in order, there are several more effective approaches than the ignore-nag-yell-punish cycle.

MAINTAIN ROUTINES

One way to arrange a consequence to misbehavior is simply to keep a steady course and continue the ordinary routines that the child's misbehavior conflicts with. The net result is that the child is inconvenienced, embarrassed, or frustrated. This chain of events need spread no further. You need not invest any energy into the matter. The child does the suffering, and the amount of suffering is enough to motivate a changed approach by the child next time. In general, maintain routines and let the child, rather than yourself or others, experience the brunt of the inconvenience:

> *"Dinner will be served at six o' clock. You have forty-five minutes to complete your chores and get ready for dinner." (Then serve at 6:00)*

> *"I'm sorry you're not ready to go with us, but you had plenty of advance notice. We're going to have to leave without you tonight; maybe next week will go better for you."*

> *"We had our family council meeting right on schedule and you chose not to attend. If you don't like the decisions we made, please come to the next meeting to express your concerns."*

Control Yourself, Not the Child

Emphasize what you will do for the child or allow, in contrast to making the child do or not do something. Refuse to cooperate with the child in the ordinary arrangement of caring services until the child decides to stop misbehaving. When the child improves in behavior, a normal exchange of affection and service between you and the child can then restart:

> *"I don't like to touch your fingers when they have been in your nose. I'll play Patty-cake with you after you wash your hands."*

 or

> *"I won't pick up your clothes when they are lying next to the hamper on your floor or have been thrown down after being washed but not worn yet."*

19

One of the most common forms of misbehavior involves an attempted display of excessive personal power in the form of an invitation to a power struggle. When you confront the child and ask the child to stop a certain misbehavior, the child digs in, becomes more blatant in the misbehavior and defies you to force a stop to the misbehavior. By this process the child lures you into a "Yes you will/No I won't" or "No you won't/Yes I will" tug-of-war. The outcome of this power struggle is almost invariably harmful to your relationship with the child. It is a "lose-lose" arrangement that should be avoided. The best procedure is to refuse to engage in the struggle. It is hard to hold a war when one of the armies doesn't show up on the battlefield. Sidestep power struggles by indicating your intent to reach a peaceable solution:

> *"I won't argue and debate with you about this. I want you to understand my real feelings and I want to understand yours. Once we really understand each other, I'm sure we can work out a reasonable solution."*

> *"When you dare me to 'make you' do this, I know something is very wrong. I'm not going to act that way toward you."*

One way children oppose disciplinary consequences is by starting a whole other set of issues. Their response to your limits becomes a separate disciplinary matter and forms a second layer of contention. Sidestep this potential power struggle and prevent this kind of expanding of the disciplinary situation. Give the child a choice of how to respond to the consequences, and avoid overcontrolling. The child's style of "accepting" the consequences of misbehavior is relatively unimportant:

> *"You must go to your room now. Are you going to walk by yourself, or do I carry you?"*

❖ *or* ❖

> *"You can dawdle as much as you want to; you're simply not coming out of this room until it's cleaned up. It doesn't matter to me how long you stay in."*

ALLOW THE CHILD TO PARTICIPATE
IN THE DISCIPLINE DECISION

The child is more likely to go along with a disciplinary consequence when it seems "fair." Give the child "a voice and a choice" in arranging the consequence:

> *"You owe ten dollars for breaking Crystal's toy. You have three choices. Either pay for it now with the money in your savings account, earn it by doing some extra work for us, or we'll give your next two allowances to Crystal. Which plan would you like to use?"*

❖ *or* ❖

> *"What do you think would be an appropriate consequence that would help you learn not to do this again and that would still be fair to you and to him?"*

22

The consequence for violating privileges is their removal until things change—usually for just a short time:

> *"Because you stayed out 15 minutes past our agreed-upon nighttime curfew, you will have to stay in tomorrow night . We'll try again on Thursday."*

or

> *"I've put the plastic bat in the garage storage cupboard because you poked Steven with it. You can have it again this Saturday if you're ready to play safely with it."*

WITHDRAW ONLY RELEVANT SERVICES

When you stop the normal exchange of services between yourself and the child, continue all other forms of cooperation that are not directly relevant to the misbehavior. Remain friendly in all other aspects and services while defining your personal limits in one area:

> *"Even though I'm not washing your clothes, I'd be happy to play a game with you now."*

or

> *"Just because I'm not driving you to go shopping doesn't mean we can't enjoy some fun food. I brought a pizza home for us tonight. Let's all dig in."*

As soon as the child has made a decision to stop the misbehavior, encourage restarting the routine exchange of services and affection:

> *"Now that you've put those clothes into the hamper, I'll be happy to wash them for you tonight."*

> *"Thank you for washing your hands. Now let me be the first to shake your hand!"*

Encourage the child to make a sincere and meaningful apology, either written or verbal, to the offended person after any misdeed. Give any needed supervision and support:

> *"Even though it was an accident, it would be best to apologize to Mr. Brown. If you wish, I'll go with you when you make your apology."*

❖ *or* ❖

> *"You owe your sister an apology for doing that. You can write it to her if you wish. I'll check with her at 8:00 and ask her whether she has been apologized to by that time."*

HELP THE CHILD TOWARD IMPROVEMENT "NEXT TIME"

When encouraging an apology, emphasize future improvements in the child's relationship with the offended person:

> *"So JoAnn will still want to play with you next time, you'd better sincerely apologize to her this evening."*

❖ *or* ❖

> *"You can't undo what you've done, but at least you can improve things for the future; you need to start with an apology."*

USE THE PRINCIPLE OF REPAYMENT

Repayment means having the child repay you and "clean up" any messes—physical, emotional, or otherwise—caused by a misdeed, whether accidental or purposeful:

> *"Here is a towel for the orange juice you accidentally knocked over. After you've wiped it up, please put the towel in the hamper."*

> *"Your delay cost me about ten minutes of my time. Please help me for ten minutes on this chore I'm doing tonight."*

ALLOW REPAYMENT THROUGH EQUIVALENT SERVICE

If the best way to pay you back is through money, allow the child to discharge the debt through work:

> *"This broken window cost $25 to fix. I'll let you work it off by crediting you at the current minimum wage for washing the car and mowing the lawn until you've given me $25 worth of service."*

> *"For ruining the pie I worked so hard to bake, you owe me a pay-back of the ingredients plus my labor. I'll let you pay it off by helping me bake a replacement pie."*

HELP THE CHILD MAKE AMENDS FOR MISBEHAVIOR

In addition to teaching the principle of repayment to you for offenses primarily involving your personal relationship with the child, teach the importance of paying back others for the pain or inconvenience that the misbehavior caused them:

> *"To mend something means to fix it with effort or work. When you make amends, you show the other persons that you're sorry and that you want to get along with them by doing them a favor to make up for the pain you caused them. What favors can you do for Joshua that will help him feel better about playing with you again?"*

> *"The best way to mend someone's feelings toward you is to pay for the pain you caused him by giving that person some joy. Do favors or good deeds for the person to show how sincere you are in wanting to make up for what you did. Apologizing was the first step; you also need to do Bruce a favor now to make up for the pain you caused him. How about taking over his household chores tomorrow?"*

27

A Final Thought

Good child discipline does not mean an endless parade of time-outs, punishments and naggings. Really good discipline involves heavy emphasis on preventing misbehavior and on confronting early, while you and the child are both relatively calm. Consequences of misbehavior are most effective when they are brief, prompt, reasonable, and logically tied to the misbehavior. Keep this booklet handy and review it often, especially during or immediately after a disciplinary situation. Review what to do next time so that gradually you adopt more and more of these techniques. As you do, your child is more likely to respond in a favorable way to your discipline and leadership, because you will be gradually strengthening your bond of love and mutual respect.